VIOLIN

MUSIC FROM A JAMES CAMERON FILM

TITANIC

D1371663

PARAMOUNT PICTURES AND TWENTIETH CENTURY FOX PRESENT A LIGHTSTORM ENTERTAINMENT PRODUCTION A JAMES CAMERON FILM "TITANIC" LEONARDO DiCAPRIO KATE WINSLET BILLY ZANE KATHY BATES FRANCES FISHER BERNARD HILL JONATHAN HYDE DANNY NUCCI GLORIA STUART DAVID WARNER AND BILL PAXTON MUSIC BY JAMES HORNER COSTUME DESIGNER DEBORAH L. SCOTT MUSIC SUPERVISOR RANDY GERSTON CO-PRODUCERS AL GIDDINGS GRANT HILL SHARON MANN FILM EDITORS CONRAD BUFF, A.C.E. JAMES CAMERON RICHARD A. HARRIS PRODUCTION DESIGNER PETER LAMONT DIRECTOR OF PHOTOGRAPHY RUSSELL CARPENTER, A.S.C. SPECIAL VISUAL EFFECTS BY DIGITAL DOMAIN EXECUTIVE PRODUCER RAE SANCHINI PRODUCED BY JAMES CAMERON AND JON LANDAU

PG-13 PARENTS STRONGLY CAUTIONED Some Material May Be Inappropriate for Children Under 13 ® Soundtrack Available on SONY CLASSICAL Read the book by HARPERPERENNIAL WRITTEN AND DIRECTED BY JAMES CAMERON titanicmovie.com DOLBY DIGITAL LIGHTSTORM ENTERTAINMENT

™ TWENTIETH CENTURY FOX. COPYRIGHT © 1998 BY PARAMOUNT PICTURES AND TWENTIETH CENTURY FOX. ALL RIGHTS RESERVED. Featuring "My Heart Will Go On" Performed by Celine Dion

A piano accompaniment book (HL00841321) is available for this collection.

ISBN 0-7935-9476-6

HAL•LEONARD®
CORPORATION

7777 W. BLUEMOUND RD. P.O. BOX 13819 MILWAUKEE, WI 53213

Visit Hal Leonard Online at
www.halleonard.com

NEVER AN ABSOLUTION

VIOLIN

By JAMES HORNER

SOUTHAMPTON

VIOLIN

By JAMES HORNER

ROSE

VIOLIN

By JAMES HORNER

UNABLE TO STAY , UNWILLING TO LEAVE

By James Horner

VIOLIN

Gently, flowing (♩ = 60)

Slightly faster (♩ = 72)

"TAKE HER TO SEA, MR. MURDOCH"

VIOLIN

By JAMES HORNER

"HARD TO STARBOARD"

VIOLIN

By James Horner

HYMN TO THE SEA

VIOLIN

By JAMES HORNER

Slowly and Smoothly (♩ = 60)

MY HEART WILL GO ON
(Love Theme From 'Titanic')

Music by JAMES HORNER
Lyric by WILL JENNINGS

VIOLIN

PLAY MORE OF YOUR FAVORITE SONGS
WITH GREAT INSTRUMENTAL FOLIOS FROM HAL LEONARD

Disney's Beauty and the Beast
8 songs from the Disney blockbuster, including: Be Our Guest • Beauty and the Beast • Belle • and more.

00850209	Flute	$5.95
00850210	Clarinet	$5.95
00850211	Alto Sax	$5.95
00850212	Trumpet	$5.95
00850213	Trombone	$5.95
00850214	Violin	$5.95

Best Songs Ever
70 of the world's favorite songs, including: All I Ask of You • All the Things You Are • Beauty and the Beast • Body and Soul • Crazy • Imagine • Let It Be • Memory • Moon River • My Favorite Things • The Rainbow Connection • Somewhere Out There • Tears in Heaven • Unchained Melody • When I Fall in Love • and more.

00841189	Flute	$7.95
00841191	Clarinet	$7.95
00841192	Alto Sax	$7.95
00841193	Trumpet	$7.95
00841194	Trombone	$7.95
00841190	Violin	$7.95

Disney Movie Magic
14 Disney favorites, including: Can You Feel the Love Tonight? • Circle of Life • Colors of the Wind • Cruella De Vil • Hakuna Matata • You've Got a Friend in Me • and more.

00841172	Flute	$5.95
00841173	Clarinet	$5.95
00841174	Alto Sax	$5.95
00841175	Trumpet	$5.95
00841176	Trombone	$5.95
00841177	Piano Acc. (for above)	$8.95
00841178	Violin	$5.95
00841179	Viola	$5.95
00841180	Cello	$5.95
00841181	Piano Acc. (for Strings)	$8.95

Evita
10 selections from the movie, including: Another Suitcase in Another Hall • Buenos Aires • Don't Cry for Me Argentina • High Flying, Adored • You Must Love Me • and more.

00120086	Flute	$5.95
00120087	Clarinet	$5.95
00120088	Alto Sax	$5.95
00120091	Trumpet	$5.95
00120096	Trombone	$5.95
00120084	Piano Acc. for above	$8.95
00120097	Violin	$5.95
00120100	Viola	$5.95
00120101	Cello	$5.95
00120085	Piano Acc. for Strings	$8.95

Disney's The Lion King
5 fun solos for students from Disney's blockbuster. Includes: Can You Feel the Love Tonight • Circle of Life • Hakuna Matata • I Just Can't Wait to Be King • Be Prepared.

00849949	Flute	$5.95
00849950	Clarinet	$5.95
00849951	Alto Sax	$5.95
00849952	Trumpet	$5.95
00849953	Trombone	$5.95
00849955	Piano Accompaniment	$9.95
00849003	Easy Violin	$5.95
00849004	Viola	$5.95
00849005	Cello	$5.95

Les Misérables
13 selections from the Broadway spectacular, including: Bring Him Home • Castle on a Cloud • I Dreamed a Dream • In My Life • On My Own • and more.

00849016	Flute	$5.95
00849017	Clarinet	$5.95
00849018	Alto Sax	$5.95
00849019	Trumpet	$5.95
00849020	Trombone	$5.95
00849021	Violin	$5.95

Best of Andrew Lloyd Webber
26 of his best, including: All I Ask of You • Close Every Door • Don't Cry for Me Argentina • I Don't Know How to Love Him • Love Changes Everything • Memory • and more.

00849939	Flute	$5.95
00849940	Clarinet	$5.95
00849941	Trumpet	$5.95
00849942	Alto Sax	$5.95
00849943	Trombone	$5.95
00849015	Violin	$5.95

Phantom of the Opera
9 songs: Think of Me • Angel of Music • The Phantom of the Opera • The Music of the Night • Prima Donna • All I Ask of You • Masquerade • Wishing You Were Somehow Here Again • The Point of No Return.

00850201	Flute	$5.95
00850202	Clarinet	$5.95
00850203	Alto Sax	$5.95
00850204	Trumpet	$5.95
00850205	Trombone	$5.95
00850207	Violin	$5.95

The Sound Of Music
11 songs: Climb Ev'ry Mountain • Do-Re-Mi • Edelweiss • I Have Confidence in Me • The Lonely Goatherd • Maria • My Favorite Things • Sixteen Going on Seventeen • So Long, Farewell • Something Good • The Sound of Music.

00850196	Flute	$5.95
00850197	Clarinet	$5.95
00850198	Alto Sax	$5.95
00850199	Trumpet	$5.95
00850200	Trombone	$5.95
00850208	Violin	$5.95

BOOK/CD PLAY-ALONG PACKS

Band Jam
Book/CD Packs
12 band favorites complete with accompaniment CD, including: Born to Be Wild • Danger Zone • Devil with the Blue Dress • Final Countdown • Get Ready for This • Gonna Make You Sweat (Everybody Dance Now) • I Got You (I Feel Good) • Rock & Roll - Part II (The Hey Song) • Twist and Shout • We Will Rock You • Wild Thing • Y.M.C.A.

00841232	Flute	$10.95
00841233	Clarinet	$10.95
00841234	Alto Sax	$10.95
00841235	Trumpet	$10.95
00841236	Horn	$10.95
00841237	Trombone	$10.95
00841238	Violin	$10.95

Favorite Movie Themes
Book/CD Packs
13 themes, including: An American Symphony • Braveheart - Main Title • Chariots of Fire • Forrest Gump - Main Title • Theme from Jurrasic Park • Mission: Impossible Theme • and more.

00841166	Flute	$10.95
00841167	Clarinet	$10.95
00841168	Trumpet/Tenor Sax	$10.95
00841169	Alto Sax	$10.95
00841170	Trombone	$10.95
00841171	French Horn	$10.95
00841296	Violin	$10.95

FOR MORE INFORMATION, SEE YOUR LOCAL MUSIC DEALER, OR WRITE TO:

HAL•LEONARD CORPORATION
7777 W. BLUEMOUND RD. P.O. BOX 13819 MILWAUKEE, WI 53213

Prices, contents, and availability subject to change without notice.
Disney characters and artwork © Disney Enterprises, Inc.

0198